A TOUR AROUND

LONDON

THOMAS BENACCI Ltd.

1	WESTMINSTER ABBEY	*11*	ROYAL MEWS	*21*	OXFORD STREET
2	HOUSES OF PARLIAMENT	*12*	APSLEY HOUSE	*22*	WALLACE COLLECTION
3	WHITEHALL	*13*	HYDE PARK	*23*	MADAME TUSSAUD'S
4	DOWNING STREET	*14*	KENSINGTON GARDENS	*24*	REGENT'S PARK
5	BANQUETING HOUSE	*15*	ALBERT MEMORIAL	*25*	REGENT STREET
6	HORSE GUARDS	*16*	ROYAL ALBERT HALL	*26*	PICCADILLY CIRCUS
7	ST. JAMES' S PARK	*17*	SCIENCE MUSEUM	*27*	SOHO
8	MALL	*18*	NATURAL HISTORY MUSEUM	*28*	TRAFALGAR SQUARE
9	BUCKINGHAM PALACE	*19*	VICTORIA & ALBERT MUSEUM	*29*	NATIONAL GALLERY
10	QUEEN'S GALLERY	*20*	MARBLE ARCH		

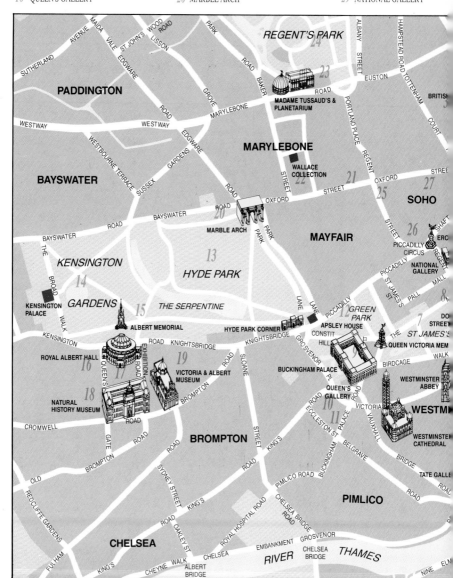

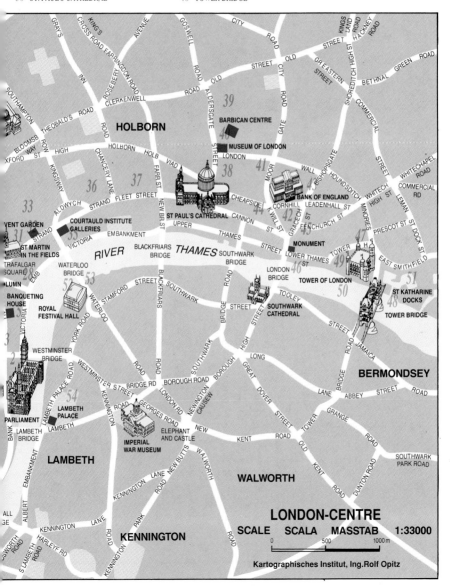

Kartographisches Institut, Ing. Rolf Opitz

3

London has nearly 2,000 years of recorded history. It was founded, as Londinium, by the Romans, following their invasion in A.D. 43. They built the first, wooden, bridge and, in A.D. 120, began the construction of the defensive walls, fragments of which can still be seen today. The Romans left in the 5th century and the city was largely abandoned, though by the 8th century it was again a busy trading centre, and in the 11th century it became the capital of England. Edward the Confessor built a palace and abbey at Westminster, thus creating the twin centres which still exist today, the government being based at Westminster while the City, which developed largely within the old walls, is the commercial and financial centre. The Norman period saw the construction of the Tower, old St. Paul's Cathedral and many churches and monasteries, as well as the first stone bridge over the Thames. Medieval London grew in importance as a trading centre and in 1215, with the sealing by King John of Magna Carta, its citizens won the right to elect their own leader, or Lord Mayor. Rapid growth during the Tudor and Stuart periods led to new building outside the walls in areas such as Lincoln's Inn and Covent Garden.

The Great Fire of 1666 destroyed three-quarters of the City and, although the rebuilding followed the Medieval street plan, the old timber houses were replaced by buildings of brick in order to reduce any future fire risk. Sir Christopher Wren rebuilt St. Paul's Cathedral and designed 51 new churches, of which 23 still stand. In the 18th century new wealth created by trade and investment led to further expansion into areas such as Mayfair, though the poor continued to live in appalling conditions. During the 19th century London spread rapidly into the suburbs, swallowing up villages and countryside, and new forms of transport were developed, such as buses and railways, including the underground railway system. Britain was then at the height of her Imperial powers, and this confidence is expressed in buildings such as the Houses of Parliament and St. Pancras Station. Large areas of London were destroyed by bombs during the Second World War and the rebuilding that followed was of mixed quality. Like all great cities, London refuses to stand still and new, often controversial, buildings continue to appear alongside the heritage of past centuries, mirroring the way the needs of the modern city co-exist with the traditions and pageantry of the past.

◄— *Houses of Parliament and Westminster Bridge*

Westminster, now the political centre of London, was, until the 11th century, a sacred place called Thorney Island, covered in brambles and surrounded by swamps. It was here that King Edward the Confessor, inspired by the churches he had seen in Normandy, decided to build a great abbey church. It was consecrated in 1065, but a week later he died and was buried in the abbey. His tomb became a popular place of pilgrimage and it is still to be found at the heart of the present **Westminster Abbey**, built by Henry III in the 13th century. William the Conqueror was crowned in the Abbey on Christmas Day 1066, and since then all Coronations have taken place here; the Coronation Chair, which has been used since 1308, can be seen in the Confessor's Chapel. Most English sovereigns were also buried here until the early 19th century, and the Abbey contains many outstanding royal tombs. The Abbey contains many other tombs and memorials to eminent men and women, but perhaps the most popular ones are those to writers, actors and musicians in Poets' Corner. One of the Abbey's chief beauties is the 16th century Henry VII's Chapel, where Henry and his wife lie beneath the most exquisite fan vaulting. Alongside the Abbey Edward the Confessor had a palace built, and from then until the time of Henry VIII the Palace of Westminster was the principal royal residence. Until the 19th century it was also the country's main court of law, and Parliament has met there since the 16th century.

Westminster Abbey

Houses of Parliament

The present **Houses of Parliament** were built after the old palace burnt down in 1834. Westminster Hall and part of St. Stephen's Chapel survived to be incorporated into the new building, designed in ornate late-Gothic style by Sir Charles Barry, with Augustus Pugin providing much of the decorative detail. The building contains the House of Commons and the House of Lords, the two chambers where parliamentary business is debated, as well as innumerable committee rooms and offices along its two miles of corridors. On the corner next to Westminster Bridge stands St. Stephen's Tower, which houses the famous 13$\frac{1}{4}$-ton bell, Big Ben, which chimes the hours. The dials of the clock are 23ft. in diameter and the minute hands are 14ft. long. A light at the top of the tower at night indicates that parliament is sitting. One of the more colourful examples of London's pageantry is the State Opening of Parliament, when the Queen, amid centuries-old ceremonial, officially opens the new session from the Throne in the House of Lords.

Whitehall

No. 10 Downing Street

In Parliament Square opposite are a number of statues to famous statesmen, including Sir Winston Churchill, who was married in nearby St. Margaret's, the parish church of the House of Commons.

The area north of Parliament Square was once covered by the sprawling Palace of Whitehall. Now **Whitehall** is a broad street lined with Government offices. In King Charles Street you can visit the underground Cabinet War Rooms, used by Winston Churchill and the War Cabinet during the Second World War. In the middle of Whitehall is Sir Edwin Lutyens' Cenotaph, which commemorates the dead of the two World Wars. In a ceremony held here every November in the presence of the Queen, wreaths of poppies are laid at the foot of the Cenotaph.

An imposing gateway now guards the entrance to **Downing Street**, named after Sir George Downing, one of Harvard's first graduates in 1642. No. 10 has been the Prime Minister's official residence since the 18th century, and the unimposing facade conceals a spacious building housing both private and official rooms. The Chancellor of the Exchequer lives at No. 11.

The only remaining part of the old Palace of Whitehall is the well-proportioned **Banqueting House**, which was built by Inigo Jones from 1619-22 in Palladian style. The impressive ceiling glorifying the monarchy was commissioned from Rubens by Charles I. Ironically it was from one of the windows of this hall that Charles stepped to his execution in 1649.

Opposite is **Horse Guards**, designed by William Kent. The mounted guard is provided by the Household Cavalry and is relieved every hour. At 11.00 (10.00 on Sunday) the colourful ceremony of Changing the Guard takes place. Through the arch under the clocktower is Horse Guards Parade, where the Trooping the Colour ceremony takes place every year on the Queen's official birthday in June.

Horse Guards

Horse Guard

Beyond is **St. James's Park**, one of London's most beautiful parks. The view from the bridge towards Whitehall is particularly pleasing and the lake is famous for its waterfowl, especially the pelicans. The park was originally enclosed as a deer park by Henry VIII. Later it was laid out for Charles II by Le Nôtre and it was remodelled again in 1829 for George IV by John Nash. With its well-tended flowerbeds and summer band concerts, the park is very popular with Londoners, and on a fine summer's day it is full of office workers eating their lunch and enjoying the sunshine.

St. James's Park

Admiralty Arch

Along the north side of St. James's Park runs the **Mall**, a wide processional route lined with plane trees, stretching from Admiralty Arch to Buckingham Palace. It takes its name from the game of "paille-maille" which was played here in Charles II's time. Overlooking the Mall are a number of impressive mansions. At the eastern end is Nash's Carlton House Terrace, now occupied by the Institute of Contemporary Art. At the western end is Clarence House, home of the Queen Mother. St.James's Palace, with its fine Tudor gateway, was built for Henry VIII on the site of a former leper hospital. Although no longer the main royal residence, ambassadors are still accredited to the "Court of St. James's".

Buckingham Palace

Queen Victoria Memorial

At the head of the Mall stands **Buckingham Palace**, the Queen's official London residence. Built in 1702-5 for the Duke of Buckingham, it was sold in 1761 to George III and remodelled for George IV by John Nash. However, it was little used by royalty until Victoria's accession to the throne in 1837. Sir Aston Webb remodelled the facade of the palace in 1913 and also designed the Queen Victoria Memorial which stands in front of it. London's most popular spectacle is Changing the Guard which takes place in the forecourt, daily in the summer and on alternate days in winter. The colourful ceremony, which is accompanied by a military band, lasts about 30 minutes.

Although it is not possible to visit the interior of Buckingham Palace, the **Queen's Gallery** holds regular changing exhibitions of works from the royal collections, and at the **Royal Mews** you can see the Queen's horses and carriages, including the magnificent State Carriage used for coronations.

The private gardens of Buckingham Palace extend to Hyde Park Corner, one of London's busiest road junctions. In the middle is the Wellington Arch, while on the north side of the island an equestrian statue of the Duke of Wellington faces **Apsley House**, which contains a collection of Wellington memorabilia, several fine rooms and some superb paintings.

Hyde Park and the adjoining **Kensington Gardens** together form one of London's largest open spaces, and provide plenty of scope for leisure activities, from horse riding along Rotten Row to boating on the Serpentine. Kensington Gardens used to be the private park of Kensington Palace, whose state apartments are well worth a visit. In 1851 the Great Exhibition was held on the south side of Hyde Park. The Crystal Palace, specially designed for the Exhibition by Joseph Paxton, was later moved to south London, where it burnt down in 1936.

Nearby is the **Albert Memorial**, unveiled in 1876 by Queen Victoria as a tribute to her consort, Prince Albert, who is shown holding the catalogue of the Great Exhibition, with which he was so closely associated.

Albert Memorial

The **Royal Albert Hall**, like the nearby museums, was built with the profits of the Great Exhibition. This vast hall, in the form of an amphitheatre, can seat up to 8,000 people, and is best known as the home of the Henry Wood Promenade Concerts.

The **Science Museum** was founded in 1856 and contains a wonderful collection of machines, scientific instruments and working models.

The **Natural History Museum** is housed in a magnificent "Romanesque" building designed by Alfred Waterhouse.

The **Victoria & Albert Museum** houses one of the world's finest collections of the decorative arts, including textiles, stained glass, sculpture, jewellery and musical instruments. Among its major treasures are the Raphael Cartoons, full-scale designs for tapestries commissioned from Raphael by Pope Leo X in 1515.

Victoria & Albert Museum

Natural History Museum

Marble Arch

Oxford Stre

In the north east corner of Hyde Park is Speakers' Corner where, on Sundays, orators are free to give voice to their opinions on almost any subject, usually accompanied by much good-natured heckling. Marooned on a nearby traffic island is **Marble Arch**, originally designed by Nash for Buckingham Palace, but moved here in 1850. It is close to the site of Tyburn, the infamous gallows where public executions were carried out until 1783. Stretching eastwards is **Oxford Street**, London's busiest shopping street, with many well known department stores. South of Oxford Street is the fashionable area of Mayfair, with its elegant squares and exclusive shops.

In Manchester Square, to the north, is the outstanding **Wallace Collection**, housed in an 18th century mansion, Hertford House. The collection is famous for its 18th century French paintings, furniture and porcelain, but also contains an impressive display of arms and armour and some fine Dutch paintings, including Frans Hals' Laughing Cavalier. Baker Street, home of Conan Doyle's fictional detective, stretches north to Marylebone Road, where you will find **Madame Tussaud's**, the popular wax museum. Here, alongside modern celebrities, you can see some of Madame Tussaud's original wax figures of victims of the guillotine, made during the French Revolution.

Nearby **Regent's Park** was laid out by Nash as part of his grand plan for the Prince Regent and is surrounded by many fine Regency terraces. Within this beautiful park are a rose garden, an open air theatre and the London Zoo.

Planetarium, Madame Tussaud's

Piccadilly Circus, the statue of Eros

Piccadilly Circus

South of Regent's Park, Portland Place leads into **Regent Street**, part of the royal route linking the park with Carlton House, the Prince Regent's residence. Nash's elegant buildings have long gone and the street now contains many famous shops, including Hamley's, the toy shop, and the mock-Tudor Liberty's. At the bottom of Regent Street is **Piccadilly Circus**, famous for its brightly-coloured illuminated signs and the statue of Eros, more correctly the Angel of Christian Charity. The London Pavilion houses Rock Circus, an exhibition about rock and pop music, and in the nearby Trocadero is the Guinness World of Records exhibition. To the west is Piccadilly, where you will find the famous store, Fortnum and Mason, and the Royal Academy of Arts, best known for its annual Summer Exhibition.

To the north is **Soho**, one of London's most colourful and cosmopolitan areas, with many foreign shops and restaurants. French Huguenots settled here in the 17th century and from then on the area has always attracted large numbers of immigrants. Among the more recent arrivals are the Chinese, who have created a community of their own in the streets around Gerrard Street. Now known as Chinatown, it has an atmosphere all its own, especially during the noisy and colourful Chinese New Year celebrations. Soho has always been a magnet for artists and writers, and many of London's best known theatres are to be found here. Leicester Square was once home to artists such as Hogarth and Reynolds; now it is better known for its cinemas.

Soho Square

A Restaurant in Soho

Trafalgar Square is famous for its pigeons, demonstrations and New Year revelries. It was laid out in 1829-41 to commemorate the great naval battle of 1805 when the French fleet was defeated by the English under Admiral Lord Nelson. The square is dominated by the 170ft. Nelson's Column, which is guarded at the base by Landseer's popular bronze lions.

On the north side of the square is the National Gallery, which houses one of the world's greatest collections of European art, with many masterpieces from the 13th to the early 20th centuries. (More modern art can be found at the Tate Gallery at Millbank). In St.Martin's Place is the **National Portrait Gallery**, which has a superb collection of portraits of famous British men and women from the Tudor period to the present day. Opposite is the church of **St. Martin-in-the-Fields**, with its striking Corinthian portico and elegant spire. Concerts are often held here, and in the crypt are a bookshop, restaurant and the London Brass Rubbing Centre.

On the south side of the square is Le Sueur's equestrian statue of Charles I, which was sold for scrap after the Civil War, but rediscovered at the Restoration and erected here in 1675. A bronze plaque in the pavement marks the official centre of London, and it was here that the original Charing Cross stood. A 19th century replacement stands in the forecourt of Charing Cross Station.

At its name suggests, the **Strand** once ran alongside the Thames, and it was lined with mansions of the nobility. Now it is better known for its theatres and hotels, but a reminder of those earlier times can be found in many of the street names and in the York Watergate in Victoria Embankment Gardens. The Victoria Embankment, built by Bazalgette in 1865-70, stretches from Westminster Bridge to Blackfriars, and is a pleasant place to walk, offering some excellent views.

North of the Strand is **Covent Garden**, one of London's liveliest quarters, with bars, shops, restaurants and open air entertainment. Originally the convent garden of Westminster Abbey, the land was later developed by the Bedford family, and Inigo Jones designed a splendid new piazza, of which St.Paul's Church is all that remains. In the 19th century the Central Market was added and Covent Garden was London's wholesale fruit and vegetable market until it moved to Nine Elms in 1974. On the east side of the piazza are the London Transport Museum and the Theatre Museum, and in Bow Street is the Royal Opera House.

Not far to the north of Covent Garden is the area of Bloomsbury, with its many literary associations. It is also home to the **British Museum**, which contains a world-famous collection of Egyptian, Assyrian, Roman and Greek antiquities, including the Elgin Marbles.

Trafalgar Square

Covent Garden

Overlooking the Thames alongside Waterloo Bridge is Somerset House, an impressive 18th century building designed by Sir William Chambers. The north wing houses the **Courtauld Institute Galleries**, another of London's major art collections. The splendid rooms, which once housed the Royal Academy, contain many old masters, but the collection is best known for its many superb Impressionist and Post-Impressionist paintings.

Further east are the Royal Courts of Justice, commonly known as the Law Courts. In the middle of the road is the Temple Bar Memorial, topped by a dragon, which marks the boundary between the City of Westminster and the **City of London**. The City, as it is called for short, covers an area slightly greater than a square mile, its boundary being much the same as that of the Roman city of Londinium. It retains many ancient institutions and traditions, yet remains an important financial and commercial centre.

Fleet Street has long been associated with printing, and was until recently the home of many national newspapers. The area has close links with the legal profession, as the four Inns of Court are all nearby. To the north are Lincoln's Inn and Gray's Inn, while to the south are Inner Temple and Middle Temple, the last two both served by the unusual circular Temple Church, which dates back to the 12th century. Another church of note in Fleet Street is Wren's St. Brides, with its famous "wedding cake" spire.

The Royal Courts of Justice

The Old Curiosity Shop

In just five days in 1666 over three-quarters of the City was destroyed in the Great Fire, which started in a bakery in Pudding Lane. Many important buildings were lost, including Livery halls, prisons, churches and old St.Paul's Cathedral. Several imaginative plans were put forward for a thorough redevelopment of the City, but, for practical reasons, the rebuilding followed the old medieval street plan. Sir Christopher Wren was the chief architect of the new City. He designed 51 new churches, but his masterpiece is **St. Paul's Cathedral**, which stands at the top of Ludgate Hill on a site where a Christian church has stood since the 7th century.

St. Paul's Cathedral

St. Paul's

The design for the new cathedral went through several versions before work started in 1675, and the building was not finished until 1709. The magnificent classical structure is crowned by the spectacular dome, whose lantern is cunningly supported by a concealed cone. Inside the dome are scenes from the life of St.Paul painted by Sir James Thornhill. Here too is the famous Whispering Gallery, where the slightest sound can be heard right round its circumference. There are many memorials in the cathedral, including those to heroes such as Wellington and Nelson, but the most evocative is the simple inscription on Wren's tomb, repeated on a stone under the dome, "Si monumentum requeris circumspice" - If you seek a monument, look around you.

Guildhall

To the north the modern **Barbican Centre** has been built on land badly damaged by bombs during the Second World War. The centre includes a concert hall, an art gallery and two theatres which are home to the Royal Shakespeare Company.

For those interested in learning about London's history, a visit to the **Museum of London** is a must, with its chronological displays of costume, paintings and excavated objects. One of the most popular displays is the 18th century Lord Mayor's Coach, which is used every November in the Lord Mayor's Show. The **Guildhall** in Gresham Street is the historic home of the Corporation of the City of London, and the Great Hall is the scene of state banquets and the annual election of the Lord Mayor.

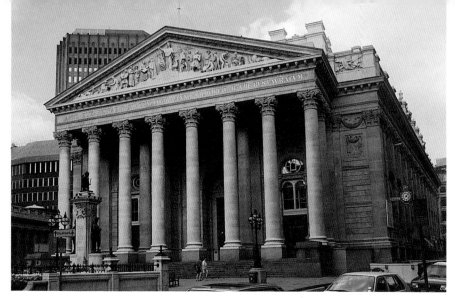

Royal Exchange

Bank of England

The heart of the City is to be found at the busy Bank intersection. To the east is the Royal Exchange, founded in 1565 by Sir Thomas Gresham. This is the third building on the site and is now occupied by the London International Financial Futures Exchange. On the north side is the **Bank of England**, popularly known as the "Old Lady of Threadneedle Street". The building was designed by Sir John Soane, though it has been much modified. The history of the Bank is told in the new museum in Bartholomew Lane.

Opposite is the **Mansion House**, which is the official residence of the Lord Mayor. Nearby are the Stock Exchange and the striking modern Lloyd's building, designed by Richard Rogers.

The **Monument** is a 202ft. column designed by Wren to commemorate the Great Fire, which broke out a short distance away in Pudding Lane. A walk up its 311 steps will give you an impressive panoramic view of the surrounding area.

At this point **London Bridge** crosses the Thames, taking you to Southwark, with its fine Gothic cathedral and theatrical associations. The first bridge here was built by the Romans, and a stone bridge was commissioned by Henry II in 1176. The 19th century bridge was sold to Lake Havasu City in Arizona and replaced by the present bridge, built between 1967-73.

Monument

The Tower of London and Tower Bridge

The **Tower of London** has been closely associated with many important events in English history and has served as citadel, palace, prison, mint and menagerie. The White Tower is the oldest part and was built in 1078 by William the Conqueror to protect the city and intimidate its citizens. Over the centuries it was much added to and by the 14th century the outer wall had been constructed. The Tower is famous for its many illustrious prisioners, such as Sir Thomas More, Sir Walter Raleigh and Guy Fawkes, and the Bloody Tower is traditionally associated with the murder of the "Princes in the Tower". Many notable people lost their heads on the executioner's block on Tower Green, including Anne Boleyn and Lady Jane Grey, and some of them are buried in the nearby Chapel of St.Peter ad Vincula. The Crown Jewels, housed in the Waterloo Barracks, include the regalia used for coronations -the oldest piece is the anointing spoon used at the coronation of King John in 1199.

The Tower is guarded by the Yeoman Warders, popularly known as "Beefeaters", who offer guided tours, clad in their traditional Tudor uniforms

Tower of London:
Beefeaters

Crown Jewels

31

Tower Bridge was designed in Gothic style to blend in with the Tower and was opened in 1894. The two massive bascules, each weighing over 1,000 tons, still open to allow ships through, though rather less frequently than in the past. The original hydraulic machinery is now housed in a museum on the south side of the bridge. The bridge is open to the public, and there are magnificent views from the upper walkway.

There are a number of other interesting places to visit within a short walk of Tower Bridge. **All Hallows by the Tower church** was rebuilt after being damaged in the Second World War, but retains a number of elements of the earlier building, including a 14th century crypt with a Roman pavement and a font cover by Grinling Gibbons. William Penn was baptised here and Samuel Pepys watched the Great Fire's progress from the tower. Opposite the Tower, moored on the Thames, is the **HMS Belfast**, a Royal Navy cruiser built in 1938 and now serving as a museum.

East of Tower Bridge are the **St.Katharine Docks**, built in 1827 by Thomas Telford, but now converted to a yacht marina and leisure centre. Some of the original warehouses have been imaginatively converted and the complex contains shops, restaurants, a hotel and the Dickens Inn pub, as well as a number of interesting boats, including Thames sailing barges.

A boat trip along the Thames is one of the best ways to see London, as it offers an excellent viewpoint from which to appreciate many fine buildings, both old and new. If you take a boat upstream from the Tower you will see many new buildings, as well as the re-developed Billingsgate Market on the north bank and the imaginative conversion of Hay's Galleria on the south bank. On either side of Waterloo Bridge are the Royal National Theatre and the **South Bank Centre**. Here you will find London's main concert hall, the Royal Festival Hall, the Hayward Gallery, which holds regular art exhibitions, the National Film Theatre and the exciting new **Museum of the Moving Image**. Further upstream is **Lambeth Palace**, which has been the London residence of the Archbishops of Canterbury since 1207.

If you go downstream from the Tower you will be able to study the extensive new development taking place in Docklands as you make your way to the historic borough of **Greenwich**, with its many maritime links. On the riverfront are the Cutty Sark, the last of the tea clippers, built in 1869, and Gipsy Moth IV, in which Sir Francis Chichester circumnavigated the world in 1966-7. The Royal Naval College was designed by Wren and it is possible to visit the Chapel and the Painted Hall, so called because of the magnificent wall and ceiling paintings by Sir James Thornhill. The National Maritime Museum houses an extensive collection illustrating Britain's maritime heritage, including the uniform worn by Nelson at the Battle of Trafalgar. The Queen's House, designed by Inigo Jones, contains an interesting collection of maritime paintings. Outside the Royal Observatory, on a hill overlooking the museum, is a line marking the zero meridian of longitude, from which time relative to **Greenwich Mean Time** is calculated.

Greenwich, Queen's House

Hampton Court Palace

To the west of London is **Hampton Court Palace**, a magnificent Tudor building set in beautiful grounds in a splendid setting by the Thames. It was begun in 1514 by Cardinal Wolsey, but was appropriated by Henry VIII, who added the Chapel and Great Hall, with its hammerbeam roof. Later Sir Christopher Wren added the south and east wings for William III. The State Apartments contain some fine period furniture and there are many splendid decorated ceilings, including several by Verrio. Also on display is a fine collection of paintings from the Royal Collection. The gardens are mostly those laid out for William III, but also look out for the delightful Pond Garden created for Henry VIII. The popular Maze is to be found to the north of the palace.

THE LONDON UNDERGROUND

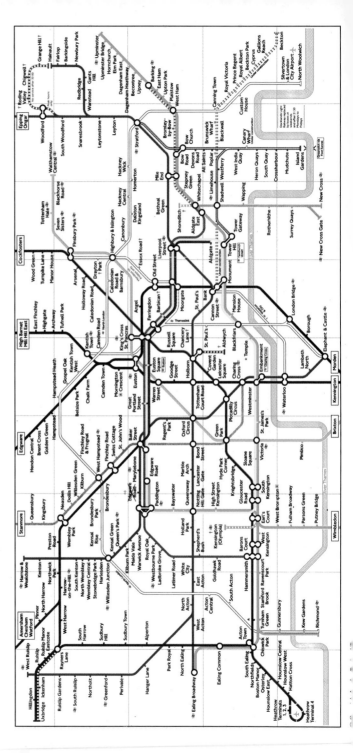